HOME
FROM THE
BANKS

Poems

Arthur William Raybold

Wigeon Publishing
San Diego

Wigeon Publishing
San Diego, California
www.WigeonPublishing.com

First Edition: August 24, 2012

ISBN-13: 978-0-9859728-4-4

Cover design by Kristine Gaitan

Cover image © Can Stock Photo Inc. / Enjoylife

Printed in the United States of America

For Suzanne

CONTENTS

HOME
FROM THE
BANKS

INTRODUCTION

Poetry is a great exercise in finding meaning in one's life by capturing moments that delight, instruct, celebrate, reward, surprise, recall, inspire, unite. As Goethe said, "And then I caught the moment fleeting. Ah! still delay. Thou art so fair." My introduction to poetry came early in life, and its influence grew as I attended school, then taught school. My mother read to me and my siblings from the Child's Garden of Verses. The lyrical phrasing enchanted me. At school, my eighth-grade English teacher, Mabel Hoyle from England, asked me and my classmates to pick a poem, memorize it, and recite it to the class. While saying aloud the lines of Robert Frost's "Mending Wall" over and over again, the sounds of the words engaged themselves with meaning.

In college, Dr. J. Bard McNulty required his students to memorize sections of Milton's "Paradise Lost." To this day, one of my favorite lines is: "Thick as autumnal leaves that strow the brooks in Valombrosia."

Writers who continue to delight me include Gerard Manley Hopkins, Dylan Thomas, Emily Dickinson, Richard Wilbur, James Joyce, Walt Whitman, the Psalmists, Henry David Thoreau, Ralph Waldo Emerson, Mary Oliver, Billie Collins, and W. S. Merlin.

Later, I taught English literature at Middlesex School, where the ninth grade was devoted to poetry. My students memorized poems and wrote some of their own. A few years ago, a student of the Class of 1964 asked me out to dinner. During the conversation he recited, without a flaw, Wordsworth's "The World Is Too Much With Us."

Poetry endures.

While at Middlesex, the headmaster encouraged me to attend the Bread Loaf School of English, a mountain-top retreat for teachers. I studied Yeats, Eliot, and Auden. I studied dramatic stage direction and played the youthful lead in "Our Town." I audited a course given by the poet John Berryman. Topping off this incredible summer, a neighbor of Bread Loaf, Robert Frost, read his poetry to a worshipful audience of English teachers. This experience best explains my first three serious poems.

After a hiatus of several decades, I began writing poems again, in part because of the death of two older siblings, both exceptional letter writers. My brother, Marshall, often regaled me with long sections from Chaucer's The Canterbury Tales, delivered in Middle English. My sister Beryl was the best-read person I'd ever known.

I wished to capture the essence of these two exceptional individuals. About that time, I also began to lose many of my high school classmates, and some of my poems reflect this.

People often ask me, how do you go about writing a poem?

Answer: I pay attention to everything I see. Subject matter is everywhere. I see my dog with three legs acting as if the loss of one leg is meaningless. I observe two wonderful family-practice physicians give up their practices because of increased administrative demands and its impact on their personal lives.

I see children dancing around gravestones, oblivious to the bodies beneath them, but thrilled with the joy of being alive. I look at old photographs and wonder if my grand-children will realize they have the power to bring me back to life. I observe pictures of ice-clad trawlers and think of Portuguese fishermen from New Bedford—men who risked their lives fishing the Georges Banks.

A classmate dies right after a high school reunion, and I begin to think of the many close friends already gone. I stop to have lunch at Rose Donuts, and Connie and Mona do not even know what a poem is. I think it curious that the younger Kennedy died in a plane crash close by where the Wampanaugs, once proud and independent, were obliterated by our forebears.

I recall my father playing Fats Waller tunes on the piano and my mother baking a lemon meringue pie. A childhood sweetheart and I argue about the temperature at which snow

2

could appear, and years later, sitting on her breezeway, I fantasize about our sailing away to some happy isles.

Through poetry, I discover greater meaning in my life—from poems not only written by others, but also those written by me that express my thoughts and observations.

It is my hope that you, too, through poetry, find greater meaning in your life and capture moments that delight, instruct, celebrate, reward, surprise, recall, inspire, unite.

Arthur W. Raybold
La Mesa, California

POEMS

ROSIE'S PRIDE

When I see Rosie's rhythmic stride
With three good legs and Beagle pride,
I wonder why my human peers
Beat their chests and shed such tears
When short-lived misery appears.

Her flapping ears are tuned to tell
This canine leads the carousel.
Despite her radiation days
That slowed her gait in many ways,
She never lost her purposed gaze.

And though her forward leg is lame,
She insists on getting in the game
By whelps and barks and jumping up,
"Open the gate for this old pup
To tumble down—don't interrupt."

BREAD LOAF 1962

I kiss you all with the bare branches

Of my winter's remembering.

Certainly, it shall smart your faces

Without the leaves of our summer's intensity.

But I do not say this to bring tears

Or mar the memory of emotion,

Only that lacking a still moving point,

I choose the next best thing —

A quick sadness, not of plaintive bird song,

But of the cracked lips of bark.

SHOTS AT QUALCOMM

Sure — flu season's here again

Can't we keep those pigs in a pen?

Ten thousand arms fling out the door

There to receive vaccines galore.

Qualcomm and Kaiser's unique spree

Puts shots in all those arms for free

Well-being clinic gone beehive

With an optimistic motto "Thrive"

Long lines found folks well-mannered.

In contrast: Bolts' fans hammered

Quiet moments in their Chevys,

Thoughts about collapsing levees.

Now the nurse with latex gloves

Takes them off to free the doves.

Historic moments such as these

Will postpone an H1 sneeze.

OF MY DOCTORS CHOU AND CHEN

Of my doctors Chou and Chen

Would they shake my hand again?

Would their diagnostic skills

Be wasted on stale admin frills?

Kaiser, are your patient millions

Nothing more than Barack's minions?

Did I lose my women MDs

Because of your physicians' fees?

Like the feds, have you misspent?

And will this now be permanent?

MY DOG AND HER GOD

My dog and her god ran down the stairs
To the hilly half acre below.
They played all day throughout the trees
Until it was time to go.

The moon made a show behind Mt. Helix
And outlined the lighted cross.
The dog and her god looked at each other
And remained at a very great loss.

The owl swooped in, a Darwinian he,
Unflappable at any novelty.
Great spans of time had made him astute
His only response was to utter a hoot.

TERESA

I find Teresa on the grass
Below the sago as I pass.
This hummingbird will never fly
Nor know the joy found in the sky,
Nor sightless beating of her wings,
No sound quite like it in all things.
I place her tiny oyster frame
Into my trembling hand lay claim.
Her bed of leaves — intensive care —
With drops of water that I share
Provides no comfort to her eyes,
Her future bleak I now surmise.
Three days I gave her all my love.
No anxious mother flew above.
I take her to a rescue place.
They look at her, laugh in my face.
"Give her to us to throw away."
Back in my yard, she passes away.
My violets lean out to Teresa,
Providing a place to release her.

NIGHTLY MAYHEM

Venus competes with two

Jets on their final approach

To Lindbergh, aided by the full moon,

As it hugs the cross on Mt. Helix.

But Tijuana's glittering lights

Steal the show even from

Sea World's polluting fireworks.

Meanwhile, only miles from my deck,

Drug wars begin their nightly mayhem

Of murder, kidnapping and beheading.

Police, bishops, mayors and Mexicans

Must pay the price for sniffing

Americans' subsistence drug habits.

Let us pray for the return of

Beatitudes — the anti-dope for sins.

Let us pray!

FUN IN THE RAIN

We had fun in the rain

Picking your fruit

Leafy, global, sensuous

And mute.

Rare moments like this

During a squall

Beat shopping at Wal-Mart

Or your neighborhood mall.

SHADOWS

The shadows of my bikes race by
And no matter how hard I try
Swerving east and sharply west
I am consistently outguessed.

Because the sun's diurnal course
Is bound by its own wry remorse
The winking spokes aloft the roof
Seem to enjoy this little spoof,

Until a cloud in silent glee
Wipes those bicycles from me.
No need to lift them from the rack
The sun refuses to come back.

CHRISTMAS AT THE BONITA CEMETERY

Sitting on the Cadwallader's stone bench

Looking at Bill and Jean's tarnished markers

After placing one lone poinsettia

Juxtaposed to Filipino overkill,

Thinking how Jean died on my watch

While William perished on Suzanne's.

Suddenly — peace interrupted — PING!

A well-hit drive from the range below.

Golfus interruptus: what possible

Linkage could be metaforged herein?

Three generations of Filipinos

Arrive at every memorial opportunity

Thanksgiving, Christmas, Easter,

Birthdays, death-days, saints' days.

Elaborate with mini-fences, pinwheels,

Photographs — keepsakes that in life

Adorned mantels, walls, nightstands,

Rear-view mirrors, and dog houses.

The children are dressed for services

But dance with spirit about the graves.

They linger for hours, eat lunch and

Polish the stones of the dear departed.

What perfect acts for Grecian urns

To capture, just as — PING! — perfect swing.

Arrested — children's dance/perfect swing.

Grecian artisans awake to this

Lustrous opportunity of melding

Calloway and memorial ritual,

While the patriarchal Anglo sits

On his in-laws' marble bench,

Wishing for dancing children.

FRUIT TO MASSACHUSETTS

As I reached each tree

They called out to me,

"Pick me, Oh please pick me."

"No," said one, not to be outdone.

"I have waited so long

For you to come along

My call is now a song:

Pick me, Oh please pick me.

My fruit is delicious

And always propitious;

Avocados don't last

The blood orange has passed.

Pick me. Oh please pick me.

The Mandarins are sweet

But not *bon appetit*.

Grapefruits are succulent

But your time is misspent.

Just look at my navel,

I will grace your table,

Pick me. Oh please pick me."

ARRIVAL

I remember your first day so well
As I left by the Nantucket bell
That went off as I left the school
To observe a delivery quite cruel.

Experiencing a Caesarian at lunch
Landed a most powerful punch!
Then out came your wonderful self,
A perfectly naked white elf.

They tore you away from my sight
Didn't see you till later that night.

When *The Matchmaker* play had ended
I removed grease from my face as amended
And ran for my old Morris Minor
Before I'd removed my eyeliner.

I leaned on my horn that late April night
Smoking a cigar with all of my might,
Surely awoke some old whaling ghosts
Listening to a young father's boasts.

PICTURE ME

Picture me on the goat cart, circa 1934

And again in my Morgan Plus 4.

So damn cute! I am aroused from the deep

As my children look at these curiously.

Sure . . . ! Put them back in the picture box

Relegate me to oblivion until happily

My grandchildren might rescue me once more.

MY KATAHDIN BUDDY

My Katahdin Buddy has passed away,
There's no one else with whom I can play
The way we did in that early June week
As dozens of moose allowed us a peek
At formidable racks plunged into the pond
That startled all living things to respond.
We'd driven from Concord to Millinocket
To immerse ourselves in the Baxter State pocket
Where wilderness and Mount Katahdin
Might take us back to that early Garden.

We set up our camp at Roaring Brook
Where bears might come and "read us the book,"
Close enough to the Ranger's Station
To ward off the Abenaki nation.
At the darkest moment, they smashed our chests
And ate all the food of their human guests.
The fright from my eyes lit up the tent
Peter often recalled with merriment.
We lay down once more as the carnivores left.
I could not sleep—of my courage bereft.

We left at dawn for remote Russell Pond;

We were deep in the woods when Pan raised his wand.

She stood in the path and seemed very tall

Her cubs made no motion — awaiting her call.

We stood and stared — it seemed like hours —

Then she turned up the hill through trees and flowers.

Up at the top, she arose and bellowed.

We moved down the path, chastened and mellowed.

When we arrived at the ranger's cottage,

We felt as though we'd made a great portage.

He'd only once met a bear on the trail,

Said we were chosen to tell a fine tale.

We stayed overnight in the Russell Pond shack;

A fire in the stove meant the bears would be back.

The latch was broken and the door banged all night.

Peter slept like a babe — no one knew of my plight.

The next day we walked to Lake Wassatacook

Tried the ranger's canoe and swam in the brook;

The ice had just melted the day before.

We no sooner dove in but we headed for shore!

As we dried our icy naked bodies,

Could there have been a better time for toddies?

If this big Marine had cardiac arrest,

Without a cell phone, he'd have gone to his rest.

Our return to base camp on that same trail

I remember clearly in great detail.

As Peter pointed out Baxter's Spotted Grouse

And the lovely birds from Maine's Audubon house,

I returned the favor by reciting Frost

About the crow that saved a day he had lost.

As we made that long trek back through the wood,

We came to know and value each other's good.

From that day forward, he was worthy of study;

And that's why I miss my Katahdin buddy.

THE FLYING CADWALLADERS

The flying Cadwalladers

Need no altimeters.

As soon as they leave the ground,

No worries! They will be found.

Their positioning devices

Cut the world into slices.

No matter if Zion

Or the elusive Orion,

They'll find their way back to earth

And qualify for rebirth.

HOME FROM THE BANKS

The ice on the draggers, home from the Banks,

After Grace Church matins, where we gave thanks,

Blindingly glistened to echo a hymn

For the fisher of men and where they swim.

My dad smoked his Lucky and watched the crew

Unload their catch and collect their due.

The hardship on boats in winter weather

Was enough to keep them working together.

So with cash in hand, they found a saloon

And drank without effort until high noon.

Their forebears, the whalers, had no such luck

As spouses saw them go round Tuckernuck.

As children, we envied these seafarers,

Believed we could compete as young darers.

Dad flicked his butt from our rusty old Ford,

Headed for home, where we knew we'd be bored.

SAY IT'S FAIRHAVEN

Why do you keep coming back they ask?

An excuse to drink and remove your mask?

To observe the remains of our once healthy class

And hope to avoid the next funeral mass?

Or to gaze once again at the marvels of Rogers

The marbled high school—the Tabatha for lodgers

The Millicent Library, the fabled Town Hall

The church Unitarian and thank God not one mall.

To think of the cash Henry gave to Mark Twain

To save our best writer from a trip down the drain.

Too bad he couldn't drill oil from a bog

To build casinos for the Wampanoag.

We wouldn't be dining in Wamsutta's domain,

But living it up with the sheiks in Bahrain.

Why do you keep coming back they ask?

Then I got serious and put down my flask.

To remember and see the people we spent

Our lives with, and how much they have meant

In homeroom and classroom and on fields of play

Where our souls began blossoming day after day

Exposed to stimuli eclectic and profound

Mr. Lawton's brain, and *Prometheus Bound*.

When the Vocal Ensemble tripped off to Hampton Beach,

We enjoyed our first freedom from our parents' reach.

The band and orchestra gave us great pleasure

And helped us mature in the arts beyond measure.

Our school's cafeteria was a welcome reprieve

And superior to hospital food, I believe.

And that bevy of beauties leading the cheers

Excelled all other classes' leaders for years.

The Senior Play revealed maturation,

But we couldn't wait for graduation

Despite the fun with the Goldsmith Follies

Bringing us together as Guys and Dollies.

And who could ever forget our five vets,

Our older role models — we owe them a debt.

Our teachers prepared us for the world of adults

Look around and observe the excellent results.

From Mr. Tunstall's down-to-earth shop

To Miss Markey's Latin, we loved every drop.

So when they ask why you keep coming back,

Say it's Fairhaven that kept us on track.

ALISON AT FIFTY

Born near the bridge of that historic town,
Along with Emerson and Thoreau of renown,
You were smart and cute and early showed poise,
At dinner you entertained the Middlesex boys.
The Cape Cod summers at Cockle Cove
Provided low tides with a treasure trove,
As well as band concerts on Chatham's Green,
And for good behavior, a Dairy Queen.
The Orleans cottage near the Outer Beach
With its little skiff made an easy reach.
Those vacation days in Williamstown,
Where we made the movie, *Charlie Brown*.
Your Worcester years were a bag eclectic,
From public to private to public — quite hectic.

You tried on each educational flavor,
Few there were that did you a favor.
The extra curricular had its appeal —
Dancing and singing were far more real.
Your ballet recital showed you'd come far,
Only exceeded by your role in "Superstar."
Your strong performance in the All Saints Choir

Gave you cathedrals where you could aspire.

You have met every challenge of family, career

And educated yourself year after year.

Kept your family together with skill and love,

Perhaps you're getting some help from above.

I am so proud of all you have done —

The best friend and daughter under the sun.

RESPONSE TO RACHAEL'S POEM

"Having fun with sweet old time"

Is why I like to play with rhyme.

As age advances to life's close,

Wise thoughts don't ride a horse called prose.

Just so — your poem was more aesthetic

Than a prosaic jumble of words pathetic.

Your use of iambic pentameter

Showed me you're not an amateur.

You solved the riddle of boy and goat

Without rocking the metric boat.

Quickly you had your eye on the prize,

Making you both practical and wise.

So Rachael enjoy your certificate,

Even if it's not magnificent.

SHIRLEY

Cocking her head to connect

She showed she had intellect.

Her spins were a great defense

To ward off Dolly's offense

And when she washed Dolly's face

She made her roll over in place.

Her scrunched up nose made her cute

In her tricolored Beagle suit

Her kisses were lavish and wet

Full of love—as good as you get.

No more she'll race Dolly below

Fight for the last avocado

No more cries of happiness

To allay my daily stress.

No more she'll lift the covers

To sleep with us mortal others.

We'll miss her sweet disposition

That seemed to be her life's mission.

FIFTY-THREE AND FIFTY-THREE

When I learned of Barbara Lawton's untimely demise

Right after our reunion's happiness wearing a disguise,

The fulcrum was now balanced at fifty-three and fifty-three,

But leveraged in favor of the dark side: don't you see?

Every visit to the cardiologist or I C U

Brings one of us a step closer to the cosmic view.

Oh classmates, how I love you more as each one passes,

Recalling bygone times of dates, sports and skipping classes.

How handsome or beautiful, newly minted for the race,

How sweetly innocent and protected by His grace,

But now the truth is out as brain cells quickly falter

The oaths we easily uttered unveiled at the altar.

Visit the remaining at their antiseptic center

And don't forget to cross yourselves before you enter.

EDWARD

He left before his birthday so early in the morn

He left without a warning and now my heart is torn.

No more his little head will fight me for the tap

No more his little body will cuddle me when I nap.

No more his raspy tongue will lick my chin so hard

No more will he attack Suzanne with whom he often sparred.

Now who will find my watches and drop them down the
   drain?

And who will make the loudest purr—unique feline refrain?

And who will hide in pillows and disappear in down?

Just when Suzanne had pills to give, Ed could not be found.

We got him Rose and Prefer and he became the boss

We love our little dogs so much and yet we're at a loss.

We'll never open cans again without expecting Ed

We'll always miss his softness and the scent around his head.

ROSE DONUTS

Next time you're at USD
And yearning for some pastry
Truck on down to Napa Street
The donuts are quite tasty.

You'll find the smiling Mona,
Serving many all so fast,
You wonder as they enter
Will there be enough to last?

Then, diminutive Connie
Rising from the lower shelves
With several pink stuffed boxes
As if filled by hiding elves.

They recite needs, ne'er spoken:
"Two lattes and one fritter,"
"One hot chocolate and a twist,"
No spills and seldom litter.

"Happy birthday! How's your dog?"
"Have you been on vacation?"
How can two Cambodians
Speak so well for their nation?

Twenty-four hours, seven days

Hard work and never a cuss,

Spreading good will every hour

Happy and ubiquitous.

More than donuts happen here

As we arrive with glum faces,

Soon affected by the joy from

These two women, modern Graces.

THIRTY-NINE

Birthdays always hurtle past

Ed and I hoped yours would last.

You and I were gone all day

Only Ed could make it stay.

Four and twenty hours select

The moment that you reflect

When you burst upon the scene,

The last child of five by Jean.

Yet your Mom and Dad recall

Is there no one else at all?

Angel watching over you

Keeps a log on what you do.

In his furry sweet delay,

Only Ed could make Time stay —

Time stood still on your birthday.

JOHN F. KENNEDY, JR.

You, John, did not read your Greek tragedy

Anymore than your father or your uncle did.

You left Fairfield, just one more Camelot

To meet your watery end off Gay Head

Not that far from Chappaquiddick.

Not even Wampanoags could find you.

Their four-hundred-year curse is still in effect

Mary Jo Kopechne for King Philip's wife.

I'm sorry you could not read the signs

You would have gone solo like Agamemnon.

OLYMPIAN EVENT

While Olympic events consumed your time,

Sister Megan Rice committed her crime

To save the world from nuclear events —

A housing shortage where we live in tents.

How could an octogenarian nun

Break into Oak Ridge without even a gun?

Compare her good crime to the NRC,

Who let San Onofre's owners go free.

Despite leaks of deadly carcinogens,

A start-up is planned by Cal. Edison.

Save up a pint, turn swords into plowshares,

Smear San Onofre, show them who cares.

THE OVERGRADUATES

The worst fate of all:

To be the redcap of culture,

Suspended between mythos and logos,

Chuckling between the Old and New Criticisms,

The bent heads and sweeping wrists,

The devotees who put it into type,

Disciplined pimps to the innocent,

Whose three months' parole

Will not quite save them

From the educator's flaccid tool.

REQUIEM

As I left my home the morning
That my sister Beryl died,
Against the budding roses
Some riotous violets cried.

"Your Beryl was a gardener
And fed us with great care.
Think not about your sorrow
But what you have to share."

Her walks through Wordsworth's country
With sheep and lakes and flowers,
Apprentice Mickey by her side,
Made many happy hours.

The words we loved of poets
From T.S. to Dickinson
Bonded us more closely
Whose hearts and souls were one.

The days we spent in high school
Close by old Buzzards Bay

Taught by England's Mabel Hoyle
Prepared us for this day.

Diminutive cheerleader
Swing-dancer without peer
Pinafore participant.
For her, art made all clear.

Her paintings and her sketches,
Original, provoking,
Arrested Prufrock on the wall;
Some embers still need stoking.

Her education knew no end
Earthbound or far above,
She spent her life with passion
In a prolonged search for love.

But now that peace has found her
(No need for us to dwell),
Quartets say, "All shall be well . . .
All manner of things shall be well."

WHOSE DOG IS ROSIE?

Ah Rosie! Where are you now?
Your rich deep soulful eyes,
Your lush multi-colored fur,
(So sweet to touch and smell),
Ears whose shapes told stories.
You barked out canine couplets.

I'm flying at forty thousand
Perhaps you are flying higher
The soul knows no bounds.
Say hello to those
Who've gone before,
As they cruise the cosmos too.

At the vet's, you gave us that last look,
"All manner of things shall be well,"
Kissed my finger and went your way.
I am not fooled by your open eyes
Now spent and your protruding tongue,
Symbols of your sight and speech.

We shall find ways to keep our bond:

Bury you beneath your avocados,

Amble along the high stone wall

You loved to jump up and walk on,

Search for your good friend the cat,

And glimpse your painting on the kitchen wall.

THANKS, MOM

The depression was in full swing
But you had a third child anyway
Reflecting your great love of having children
Though some of us may not have loved you for it.
Thanks for monitoring my homework
Making sure I made the honor roll.
Drilling me in Latin vocabulary
Coaching me on my English papers
Making me take dancing lessons.
Encouraging me to play the clarinet
Under the eye of Archie Messenger
So that I got to play in the town band!
Thanks for moving to Mattapoisett
With the ghosts of the Wampanoags,
Balloon fish, snapper blues and quahogs,
Dave Jenney — troubadour and yachtsman
Plying the waters of Buzzards Bay
In his tidy wooden dory
To Weepecket, Naushon, Angelica Point.
Throwing the ball skyward in Shipyard Park
Caring for Miss Batelle's lawn and garden
Using her lumber from the mansion
To build my chicken house and rabbit run

And our beach shack at Strawberry Point.

Playing six-man football at Center School

Riding Mahoney's truck at the football rallies.

Dating those summer girls — Nancy and Carol

Teaching swimming and tennis at Pt. Connett.

Creating the "Scuttlebutt" luncheonette

In the back of Lebaron's Variety Store.

Serving hotdogs and hamburgers on Wed. nights

To the joyous square dancers on Straight Wharf

And to Saturday's rapt band concert crowd.

Rowing out to the N.Y. Yacht Club fleet

Taking orders from the not-so-fast menu,

Rowing out again to deliver their lunches,

Talking politics with the Scuttlebutt gang.

Thanks, Mom, for those Norman Rockwell years.

SOAP OPERA

A new bar of soap

Gives one instant hope

That new days are born

Goodbye to forlorn.

Until put to use

Without much abuse

It began to shrink

Quite subtly I think.

Its earthly demise

Caught me by surprise:

Wham! A metaphor —

Like life — what's it for?

It hastens toward death

Takes away our breath

I wonder what's next —

I reach for the Text.

Good luck — typecasting

Life everlasting.

Scraps back in the tray

On your knees and pray.

BILLY SYLVESTER

Billy Sylvester just won't lie down,

Despite his valor and general renown.

He left us lamblike and disappeared,

But lately came sounds that Julie feared,

Such as cracking noises about the roof,

As if he might enter, but remained aloof.

Billy's passion for Julie knew no bounds —

One lustful look — you'd be thrown to the hounds.

His culinary skills set Julie on fire,

Designed to move her to his desire,

Their feasting table became their bed,

They tore off their clothes and each other fed.

Be it known that this table now emits sounds

That Julie knows means Billy is around.

COMMUNION

Was there something that you missed
By not taking the Eucharist?
Why did you refuse the host?
Out of favor with the Ghost?
You went to every Sunday mass.
Kneeled down but said, "I'll pass."
You served lunch to your seniors,
Just as to Sigmas in the lean years.
We went east to find the traces
Of King Phillip's hiding places.
Plymouth, Taunton, Narraganset—
Soaked up the signs, not to forget.
You gave your wife your hospice care,
Fed and bathed her, said a prayer.
When cancer struck, you gave again;
I spooned you food up until the end.
After the funeral, the Father said,
"Why did John not take the bread?"
I would not say consubstantial
Because John loved the ritual.
So, my pre-divinity friend,
The mystery lives without end.

NICOLINA

A small dog placed an ad in the Union-Trib:

Two families have poked a hole in my rib.

The children are mean and pull on my ears.

They shout obscenities until I shed tears.

I live in Santee on New Bedford Place,

Just a block or two from Providence Trace.

Come before noon when no one's at home.

I'll be hiding inside a bumper of chrome.

I have no playmates and am left alone.

My red-and-white coat and pleading brown eyes,

Red eyelashes will take you by surprise.

Jump the chain fence, behave like a snake.

Together we'll pull off a prison break.

Rescue me, dear friend; we'll be mates forever,

Regardless which of us wears the tether.

GALATEA AT ANCHOR

My chicory morning walk with Ann
By Rosa Rugosa shrubs began,
While studious egrets stalked their prey
And eels lived not to talk that day.

My Angelica stroll with Carol
Out to rocks and sand too narrow
Brought us to the Point—take stock:
Too late to talk of shoals and rock.

My evening sail with Nancy
In a Beetle Cat—nothing fancy
Brought back the Padanaram Races
We won as we left them in their traces.

Yet, Galatea gently rolled;
Her story still remains untold.
While Mate and Captain traded quips,
Their wives made jam of Rosa's hips!

ALANNA AT SEVENTY

From early days to just last week,
You've always given me a peek
Of your most recent work of art.
Of all of them, I've felt a part.
I knew your skills ran very deep
And your desires would make the leap.
Your grit in getting into Tuller
Gave proof your efforts would be stellar.
Your need to go to France that summer
Confirmed your choosing your own drummer.
Your confidence became apparent,
No stopping this emergent talent.
Drawing, sketching, painting, learning,
Pursuing your path — never turning.
Searching for that certain image;
Seeing with your mind that image.
Your figures, landscapes, unique prints,
Providing imagistic hints.
Now at this time of maturity,
You have come to a new certainty.
I've followed your metamorpho, sis,
And know you've received the muse's kiss.

LEO IN THE MORNING

Leo, reverentially absorbed
By the magazine he touches and
By the tulips that touch him,
Leans into the captured moment
With the other players
Seen or unseen,

While the waiting outdoors,
Always patient,
Sees him in a larger context
Than that framed by the artist.
A benevolent mythology
Holds Leo's younger
Self intact.

DEATH CAME TO MY ADDRESS BOOK

Death came to my address book
Just when the grim reaper's hook
Tore them away to Banish
Just down the road from Vanish.
It appeared harmless to me
Like carving names on a tree
To place them in a new tract;
The first was dog-eared in fact.
Was I the agent of the Fates
By recording their birth dates?
I have ceased to add more names,
I refuse to play these games.

UP UNTIL NOW

When I was very young, my sister cared for me;
She dressed me to the nines and scrubbed my dirty knees.
She didn't need a doll or a dress-up party;
She was an able mini-Mom with little sibling Artie.

She took me to the park and showed me how to swing
And how to feed the pigeons, which liked to hear me sing.
Later when I went to school, the teachers knew of Beryl;
They said I'd better shine by God or drop out at my peril.

Life was made quite simple with her to pave the way,
But Beryl went to RISD — then I began to pay.
I missed her windup portable that played Glenn Miller greats
And tunes from Oklahoma that spoke out from 78s.

Most I missed the dancing and my sister's jitterbugging
While I learned how to waltz and how to dance while
    hugging.
Then along came Prescott, the handsome architect,
A World War II navigator, lean and circumspect.

All this time our Candace was waiting in the wings
To make a timely entrance — "Soul clap its hands and sing."
Not to be upstaged by primogeniture,
Enter Shere and Jaime to make their place secure.

Time and distance took their toll; long silences ensued.
Then Beryl wrote her brother, and friendship was renewed.
Much maligned, the letter became the means of choice
By which our thoughts could find a true and honest voice.

Sorry, girls, you live so close and only get dessert
The entrées are rich and varied — a cerebral alert:
Essays like her postcards, startling creative birds,
In shapes like her own pottery — flesh made into words.

Have you ever walked with Beryl? She "seeks a newer world,"
A swinger of those birches, communing where'er she's hurled.

MADELINE

Madeline came to our house to enjoy a salmon dinner;

Like all other three-year-olds, she wants to be a winner.

So she climbed down the old stone stairs and started digging holes.

My three beagle girls followed her to see the flashing poles.

No sooner had she excavated some nifty little cavities

But she began to bury beagle toys — an innocent depravity.

When the corn and the asparagus and salmon were consumed,

The dogs went back down to see if their deposits had been doomed.

Nothing was amiss as they unearthed their fuzzy treasures,

But something ghostly bothered them because of these measures.

They shook the objects clean and licked them until purified.

Maddie looked down upon them, as if she were mystified:

Our diminutive priestess raised her arms to give a sign;

The dogs bowed repectfully, knowing she was benign.

EXACTLY LIKE YOU

My Dad's old upright in the dining room

Was not designed for music *summa cum.*

Though 'twas a respite from Copper & Brass

And on the weekends an acre of grass,

My Mother's sour look when the notes began

Stated his repertoire was also-ran:

"Sit right down and write myself a letter" —

"Oh Lord! Can't you think of something better?"

And in response came, "Exactly like you."

"Oh, please stop that noise; you're banging your shoe."

With four kids and no longer a flapper,

She felt the Twenties could only entrap her.

Playing the organ to the Baptist pews

Gave him more clout than playin' the Blues.

"Arthur — stop playing and come to dinner."

He knew he was not Fats Waller, a winner.

But when Mom went with friends to play canasta,

Dad played those jazz songs just like the Master.

MY BROTHER MARSHALL

You had a hell of a go at it.

Getting lost in the fog in New Bedford harbor,

Bicycling from Buzzard's Bay to New Hampshire,

Breaking your arm on the day the doctor was fishing,

Looting the beaches after the '38 hurricane,

Enjoying the best paper route in Fairhaven,

Scooping the news of Pearl Harbor on your crystal set,

Working at Hutchinson's Bookstore,

When other boys were playing football.

Making model airplanes out of balsa and glue,

That in later years became reality.

Working at Camp Otis as a carpenter,

Before joining the Army Air Corp at 18.

Trying to become a pilot and a warrior

Before the last good war was ended.

Going through Dartmouth in three years

And rejoining the U.S. Air Force so

You could airlift those dying GIs out of Seoul

To Tachikawa Air Base in Tokyo,

Where you attended the University.

Returning to nouveau Shaker Heights,

Where your taxi was *persona non grata*.

Rebounding to the University of Mexico
And into the classroom at Marblehead High.

Living with American Indian tribes so you
Could come to understand their simpler culture.
Flying for the National Chinese Air Force
Prior to the Communist takeover of China.
Teaching the Argentine Air Force boys to fly
American multi-engine aircraft.
Developing a system for roulette
And perfecting it daily in Monte Carlo.
Learning five foreign languages
So you could teach skiing in many tongues.
Living in Haight Ashbury with the hippies,
Specializing in moving all your earthly
Possessions in five minutes and be on your way.
Teaching disabled children how to ski in Santa Fe,
Driving for a messenger service
Though you were now blind in one eye.
Falling on the ice while running to
Recuperate from a ski accident.
Having holes drilled in your skull,

Not being able to ski or drive.

Fed by charity Meals on Wheels.

Exiting this world with a

Couple of vodkas and a plastic bag

Was your way of passing from this

World to the next without

Burdening us or the state.

As a member of the Mayflower Society

And the Hemlock Society,

You were totally self-sufficient and

Spent your time here

"Chasing life into a corner."

OFF BY DEGREES

If I picked up the *Standard Times* one day

And it said Anne Stowell had passed away . . .

She walked down Beacon Street to the beach.

In a way, I knew she was out of reach

So instead I spoke to her of snow

You could only have it around thirty or so.

She responded coolly I was off by degrees

And when would I get down on my knees?

45TH REUNION

The passion of our Beacon Hill youth
Gives way to one more precious hour
When we watch feeding goldfinch
Brilliant in the Mattapoisett rain.

Why do we talk *Presto Press*
And Miss Batelle's remodeled house,
When dancing begonias
In your perfumed breezeway
Prompt some psychic burst
Of love for time remembered?

Shall we not in this
Sweet aging friendship
Walk down Ship Street, hand in hand,
Embark one moonlit night,
Standing astern some wooden "cat"
As Old Rochester breezes
Whisk us off to an Elizabethan isle?

THE SMOKE THAT ROSE

As the hot ash fell from Dean Hood's lips

The now dark classroom echoed his quips:

"From morn to noon, a summer's day He fell;

A piece of God descended into Hell."

"No, sir, not God," the naive pre-div said.

"When he quit God, he was no longer God."

The Dean lit up another cigarette.

The match revealed a face that showed regret.

His title was rescinded long ago,

When he refused to play quid pro quo

The legacy did not get to attend,

The monies for the quad came to an end.

Dean Hood's class in Argument and Debate

Received a bad rap—why would one tempt fate?

Assignments were tough and all-consuming;

He used satire as part of his grooming.

One day, unprepared, out of my habit:

"Raybold, stop acting like a half-screwed rabbit."

Years later, whether in business or teaching,

I realized Hood's effect was far-reaching.

The smoke that rose from his deep scrutiny

Made me pursue all hubris with mutiny.

WHAT'S LIKE ...

My dog's licking the raindrops
Running down the outside pane?
Man's thirsting for the afterlife;
The left-behind will remain.

Is it really out of reach
Despite all of God's teasing?
No liturgy can bridge the gap
No matter how God-pleasing.

Now that Nature's stopped the rain,
Nicki's short-lived rapture
Gives us insight into just how hard
It is for God to capture.

TO CAROL, BREAD LOAF 1962

At first I thought it was Carol

Decked out in Emily's apparel;

Hidden Eros had moved in again

With latent indifferent aplomb.

But now that the set has been struck,

It's *agapē* with which I have truck.

And what I feared catatonic

Has been reduced to platonic.

TO EMILY, BREAD LOAF 1962

You remind me of my first love

And also of my last.

You remind me of a present

That's now become a past.

Don't say, "The moonlight's terrible,"

I find the words unbearable.

Or, "Goodbye to clock's ticking,"

My heart and throat are sticking.

You remind me I'll forget you

That we'll be weaned away

To the absolute unearthly

And so we start today.

ABOUT THE AUTHOR

Arthur Raybold grew up in New England and graduated from Trinity College (B.A.) and Columbia University (M.Ed.). He taught English at Nantucket High School, served as Chairman of the English Department at Middlesex School in Concord, Massachusetts, and later became involved in public education, creating special teacher training programs in Worcester, Massachusetts.

After a career in education, Raybold took his teaching and writing skills to the business world. He lives near San Diego with his wife, Suzanne Cadwallader, and their three beagles, Prefer, Dolly, and Nicolina. Raybold is the Vice President of Business Development for a local company.

Besides writing poetry, his interests include politics, travel, bicycling, rescuing beagles, and hiking.

ACKNOWLEDGEMENTS

I found inspiration from my children when they were very young for "trailing clouds of glory as they came." Once, when putting three-year-old Alison to bed, I asked innocently, "Where did you come from?" Without hesitation, she replied, "I come from God." My five-year-old son Tersh was being driven to school by the headmaster's wife, Judy Sheldon, when he said, "Tiger! Tiger! Burning bright / In the forests of the night / What immortal hand or Eye / Could frame thy fearful symmetry?"

I began to look at my poems from an artist's perception thanks to my sister Alanna Fagan, a recognized Milford, Connecticut, portrait, landscape, and interior design artist. Her critiques were most helpful as we discussed the often parallel process of writing poetry and painting people and landscapes.

We rarely thank our parents for all they do for us, so I finally get my chance. My mother let me keep baby chicks in the house until they were old enough to be put in coops outside. She edited my writing assignments so my teachers would be pleased. She convinced me to take clarinet lessons.

My dad entertained us by playing Fats Waller tunes, and he would play music if we simply whistled the notes. As a ninth grader, I became the first boy on the football team to have a pair of low-cut cleats. He called me Sport, and the only time I ever scored a touchdown he became so excited he fell out of the stands.

I am grateful to my longtime friend Kristine Gaitan, who agreed to create the cover for this book. Her countless hours spent searching for the right picture in which to wrap the book with a design that captured my intent will be long appreciated.

Finally, I thank my dear friend, Larry Edwards, for introducing me to the Laguna Mountains, where we could hear nothing but the sounds of birds and an occasional poem recited by me. Larry agreed to publish my first book of poetry and in the process has made countless positive suggestions.

CPSIA information can be obtained at www.ICGtesting.com
Printed in the USA
LVOW06s1539281013

358941LV00001B/236/P